To

Pammykins

From

Sharon

With a Heartful of Love

Date

February 27, 2018

May these gentle musings on life and God

And these pearls of wisdom from Proverbs

Brighten your day and

Illuminate your path.

Anita Higman   Ruth Vaughn

A

Collection

of Pearls

Inspiration

and Wisdom

HOWARD
PUBLISHING CO.

$\mathcal{O}$ur purpose at Howard Publishing is to:
- *Increase faith* in the hearts of growing Christians
- *Inspire holiness* in the lives of believers
- *Instill hope* in the hearts of struggling people everywhere

$\mathcal{B}$ecause He's coming again!

Pearls © 2002 by Ruth Vaughn and Anita Higman
All rights reserved. Printed in the United States of America

Published by Howard Publishing Co., Inc.
3117 North 7th Street, West Monroe, Louisiana 71291-2227

02 03 04 05 06 07 08 09 10 11   10 9 8 7 6 5 4 3 2 1

Edited by Chrys Howard and Philis Boultinghouse
Interior design by Stephanie Denney
Cover design by LinDee Loveland

ISBN: 1-58229-225-6

Unless otherwise noted, the proverbs quoted are from the *Holy Bible,* New Living Translation, copyright © 1996. Used by permission of Tyndale House Publishers, Inc., Wheaton, Illinois 60189. All rights reserved. Scripture quotations marked NIV are from the Holy Bible, New International Version. Copyright © 1973, 1978, 1984, by International Bible Society. Used by permission of Zondervan Publishing House. All rights reserved. (Some line breaks and initial-letter capitalizations were added.)

to beloved granddaughters,

Ashley and Kourtney

—Ruth

to beautiful daughter,

Hillary

—Anita

Sit for a minute and pay attention to
   what sounds like nothing at all.
Perhaps there is only a hint of a breeze
   making the pine needles wave
Or a bird skipping across a wisteria-covered
   fence;
But it is in the stillness that God calls you
   to watch and listen.
It is in silence that you can best hear the
   majestic voice of God.

Listen to me! For I have...

Everything I say is right,

every kind of deception. My...

There is nothing crooked or...

to anyone with understanding...

learn. "Choose my instruction...

edge over pure gold." ... Listen to...

to tell you. Everything I say...

and hate every kind of decep...

good. There is nothing crooked...

plain to anyone with unders...

to learn. "Choose my instruct...

knowledge over pure gold."...

Listen to me!
For I have excellent things to tell you.
Everything I say is right, for I speak the truth and
   hate every kind of deception.
My advice is wholesome and good.
There is nothing crooked or twisted in it.
My words are plain to anyone with understanding,
Clear to those who want to learn.
"Choose my instruction rather than silver,
And knowledge over pure gold."

Proverbs 8:6-10

$\mathcal{F}$or budding trees that bring
splendor to winter-barrenness,
For pole-vaulting leaps of faith,
For serendipity-somersaults of joy,
For the new beginning of every
dawn,
And, once in a while, for the
reality of heaven on earth—
I thank you, Lord.

It is the glory of God to conceal a
  matter;
To search out a matter is the glory of
  kings.

Proverbs 25:2 NIV

Today, limit your comments to uplifting remarks and see what happens. Maybe you will receive a pleasant surprise in return!

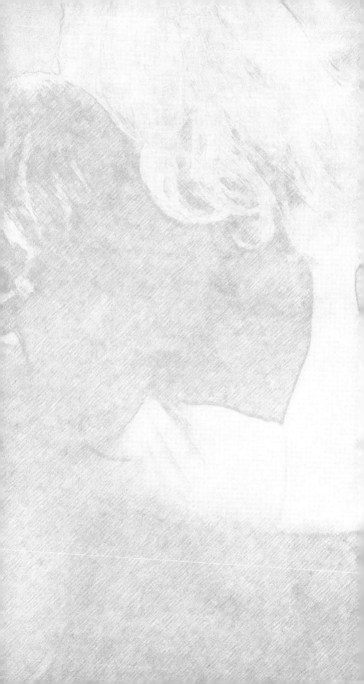

Kind words are like honey—
Sweet to the soul and healthy for the body.

Proverbs 16:24

Who am I?
It is a question often asked in deep soul-study.
When you looked in the mirror this morning,
Whom did you see in the reflection?
Was it Florence Nightingale,
Anna Pavalova, Louisa May Alcott,
Or maybe Anne of Green Gables?
Are you the girl who burns the candle at both ends?
Are you your mother's dream come true?
In truth, you are all of these,
But there is a more fundamental answer:
You are God's special creation,
His delight in all of life's seasons.

My child, don't ignore it wh
don't be discouraged when he
those he loves. Just as a fath
delights. My child, don't ign
you. And don't be discouraged
Lord correct... he loves. J
whom he de... My child
disciplines you, And don't be
For the Lord corrects those he
hild in whom he delights.
Lord disciplines you, And do
you, For the Lord corrects tho
ects a child in whom he del

My child, don't ignore it when the LORD
   disciplines you,
And don't be discouraged when he
   corrects you.
For the LORD corrects those he loves,
Just as a father corrects a child in whom
   he delights.

Proverbs 3:11-12

The nicest thing about
a friendly greeting
Is that it's a gift that all
folks like to receive
And every person can
afford to give.

A cheerful look brings joy to the heart;
Good news makes for good health.

Proverbs 15:30

*A*nother birthday...
A Kodak moment filled with laughter and love.
As you age, you will discover that knowing what
    you need
Is more important than knowing what you want.
It's a kind of clear-eyed wisdom
That allows you to see what is worthless
And what is valuable.
It's touching someone you know will never turn
    away.
It's reaching for a future that's really worth the
    climb.
It's learning to let go of the past
And run with the glories of the present.

Don't turn your back on wisdom, her, and she'll guard you, she will protect you. Love her, turn your back on wisdom, For and she will guard you. Don't will protect, Love her, an your back, For she will guard you. Don't turn yo protect you. Love her, and sh back on wisdom, For she will guard you. Don't turn your ba you. Love her, and she will g wisdom, For she will protec

Don't turn your back on wisdom,
For she will protect you.
Love her, and she will guard you.

Proverbs 4:6

Kindness is underrated.
The world is full of people with the kind
 of talents that razzle-dazzle—
Those public kind of gifts that everyone
 notices.
But what about kindness?
Kindness will never be listed on the stock
 exchange,
And it doesn't make it onto the covers
 of prestigious financial magazines.
It won't win the gold or even get a
 standing ovation.
It just rests at the feet of Jesus with His
 full favor.

Kindness, with its simple but majestic
  beauty,
Changes the lives of every human
  it touches.
It is a daily miracle.
We each have the choice to possess it
  in abundance
And to give it freely and wholeheartedly.

Never let loyalty and kindness get away from you!
Wear them like a necklace;
Write them deep within your heart.

Proverbs 3:3

Climb the hills through
yesterday
And remember laughing
merrily as you ran to keep
up with someone who
possessed a stronger, longer
pace.
Feel the cool breeze as you
embrace a park swing and
push yourself toward the sky.
Recapture the gasp of relief as
arms reach to rescue you at
the end of a silver slide.
Celebrate childhood like
confetti tossed on an
emerald-colored lawn.
We all grow up, but the
magic lives on forever.
As you pause to visit the
engravings on your heart,
Whisper, "Thank You, God,
for yesterday."

Gray hair is a crown of glory;
It is gained by living a godly life.

Proverbs 16:31

The carefree days of childhood
  are filled with
Laughter, dancing, and singing.
Of course, it isn't really that simplistic.
Early on, we learn that a lot of life is hard.
But if we choose to face life with God,
Then we can always laugh,
Always sing,
And always dance.

My child, listen to me and treasure my instructions.

Tune your ears to wisdom,

And concentrate on understanding.

Cry out for insight and understanding.

Search for them as you would for lost money or
hidden treasure.

Then you will understand what it means to fear the
LORD,

And you will gain knowledge of God.

Proverbs 2:1-5

O God . . . You who love,
Come and sit with me while I cry.
I know Your presence will give me
Courage to smile tomorrow.
Only You and I will know
I cried tonight.

The lamp of the LORD searches the spirit of a man;
It searches out his inmost being.

Proverbs 20:27 NIV

Look at your hands.
They look much like everyone
    else's hands. . . .
And yet on closer inspection,
    they are wonderfully unique.
Think of it.
No other fingerprints are just
    like yours in all this vast
    earth!
Fascinating!
What Great Engineer could
    put all this together?
God, in His divine wisdom,
    chose to make each of us
    an awesome and precious
    wonder.
All our own.

By wisdom the LORD founded the earth;
By understanding he established the heavens.

Proverbs 3:19

Have you ever heard the expression
"Being groomed for the top"?
Men and women, boys and girls who are
   recognized for their gifts in a certain field
   are given special assistance to advance
   quickly.
It's really quite an honor.

But do you feel honored when God grooms
   you for the top?
Are you thankful for the challenging nudges
   and constant polishing?
God's is a different sort of grooming,
And heaven is certainly a more magnificent
   kind of top!
Do you welcome His daily attention?
Do you always give Him your best?
Are you yielded to this grooming?

My child, don't lose sight of

Hang on to them, for they f

honor and respect. They keep

your feet from stumbling. Yo

enjoy pleasant dreams. You

destruction ... upon

security. ... keep your

Do not withhold good from th

your power to help them.

planning and insight. Hang

with life and bring you hono

n your way and keep your f

town without fear and enjoy

My child, don't lose sight of good planning
and insight.
Hang on to them, for they fill you with life
and bring you honor and respect.
They keep you safe on your way and keep
your feet from stumbling.
You can lie down without fear and enjoy
pleasant dreams.
You need not be afraid of disaster or the
destruction that comes upon the wicked,
For the LORD is your security.
He will keep your foot from being caught in
a trap.
Do not withhold good from those who
deserve it
When it's in your power to help them.

Proverbs 3:21-27

There's a gentle breeze nudging you to
  hold on to your dreams,
To forget yesterday and reach for new visions
  with a prayerful heart.
Only in obeying these breeze-whispers
Will you find the courage for new challenges.
Rejoice, and be glad.
Obey.
Why?
Because God is the voice of the
  whispering breeze.

Follow my advice, my son;
Always treasure my commands.
Obey them and live!
Guard my teachings as your most precious
  possession.
Tie them on your fingers as a reminder.
Write them deep within your heart.

Proverbs 7:1-3

Keep watch on your friendships
so that the shine doesn't rub off.
Like old silver, they will glisten with the
polishing agent called "listening."
Got any friendships you need to put the
shine back on today?

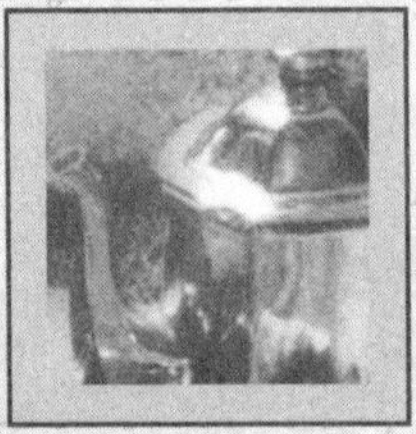

As iron sharpens iron,
A friend sharpens a friend.

Proverbs 27:17

*D*o you sometimes wonder if God remembers you?

Are you worn out from asking?

Are you weary from doubting?

Are your knuckles bleeding from knocking on doors that remain steadfastly closed?

Know this: He never forgets.

He sees your pain.

He honors your efforts.

In time, the asking, seeking, and knocking will be acknowledged.

He promised.

Trust in the LORD with all your heart;
Do not depend on your own understanding.
Seek his will in all you do,
And he will direct your paths.

Proverbs 3:5-6

This new day is a spotless,
  shining thing,
Fresh as the breath of spring.
I can choose to fill this day
  with lovely thoughts,
Kindly helpful deeds,
Forgetting myself in concern
  for others' needs.

Oh Lord, help me use this
  day for You.

If you help the poor, you are lending to the
LORD—
And he will repay you!

Proverbs 19:17

I thank You, Lord, for Your sunshine.
But no less thankful am I for Your storms.
For it is then that I cling more tightly to Your hand
And lean upon Your strength.
I ask only that I shall be able to yield myself—
Without reservation—
To Your hand,
So that You can do with my life
What is best and what brings glory to Your Name.

Commit your work to the LORD,
And then your plans will succeed.

Proverbs 16:3

On days when you think your spiritual
   growth is hopelessly slow in flourishing,
Remember that the gargantuan oak tree
   and the majestic redwood grew silently,
   slowly—imperceptively.
They grew and stretched magnificently—
   even when no one seemed to
   notice. . . .
Except for the caring and watchful eye of
   the Master Caretaker.

Wisdom is a tree of life to those who embrace her;
Happy are those who hold her tightly.

Proverbs 3:18

$\mathcal{L}$ife gets so busy-busy-busy-busy
That I forget I need You.
Sometimes You have to trip me,
So I fall flat.
And then I remember I need You.
Thank You for picking me up and
   loving me still.

In his heart a man plans his course,
But the LORD determines his steps.

Proverbs 16:9 NIV

You are forgiven.
Three of the sweetest words ever
    spoken.
What delight!
What release, what soaring joy!
These three simple words have the
    power to bring honor,
Freedom,
And hope.
These are words we long to hear
And need to graciously extend:
You are forgiven!

Wisdom is sweet to your soul.
If you find it, you will have a bright future,
And your hopes will not be cut short.

Proverbs 24:14

Sometimes my faith is as sturdy as an iron gate.
But at other times, it is as flimsy as an
Old slip wanting to fall around my ankles.
What kind of faith will I have today?
Amazingly, the choice is up to me.

She is clothed with strength and dignity,
And she laughs with no fear of the future.

Proverbs 31:25

Today, kneel in prayer with
a friend or for a friend.
God knows how deeply we,
    His children, need each other.

God, bless our friendships.

The heartfelt counsel of a fri

ncense. Never abandon a frie

Them in your time of need, you

for assistance. It is better to

who lives far away. The hea

as perfume   se. New

your father   in your t

your relatives for assistance.

than to a relative who lives f

friend is as sweet as perfume

friend—either yours or your f

you won't have to ask your re

to go to a neighbor than to a

The heartfelt counsel of a friend is as sweet
as perfume and incense.

Never abandon a friend—either yours or
your father's.

Then in your time of need, you won't have
to ask your relatives for assistance.

It is better to go to a neighbor than to a
relative who lives far away.

Proverbs 27:9-10

When we reach toward heaven, we connect
    with Someone greater than ourselves.
Thankfully, there is much more than clouds and
    air and dreams to touch.
There is a Great Designer who not only wants
    connection,
But who loved us enough to pay the price
For a glorious bridge to heaven.